A Kind of Amnesty Given the Mind

A Kind of Amnesty Given the Mind

Unfolding a Part of the World View of the Archangel

A Novelette in Verse by Dicko King

Grid Books

GRID BOOKS
Boston, Massachusetts
grid-books.org

Cover art by Treva Maulhardt.

Author photo by Chris Bailey

I am ever grateful to Elizabeth Murphy and Dan Carey of Grid Books for the close reading and care they gave in editing this manuscript, and to their devotion to independent publishing, to the press, and to its authors.

Gratitude as well to the authors Cynthia Manick and Brandi George for their early critiques, edits, and suggestions of this manuscript.

Printed in the United States. Book design by Michael Alpert

ISBN: 978-1-9468304-0
LCCN: 2025936676

To my little brothers

TABLE OF CONTENTS

WATCH & WARD

A NATURAL SCENE

OFFERED TO GOD

A Kind of Amnesty Given the Mind

Dis laudes qui hilaratus adulescentia mea.
Praise to the gods who gladdened my youth.

Feck'less. (fĕk'lĕs), a. [Perh. A corruption of *effectless*]
Spiritless; weak; worthless. (Scot.)

Fecks. (fĕks), *n.* A corruption of the word *faith*. *Shak.*
–*Webster's Revised Unabridged Dictionary*
of the English Language, 1913

BEFORE BEGINNING AT THE BEGINNING

I'll Create the Creation Story in a Minute or When I Get Around to . . .

This is built around a little-known historical event

I'll say this up front:

I am more the god of small round tumours formed around wasp eggs
than the god I want to be—the godhead of jams and jellies and a town in
S. New York, pop: around 12,345—and of which I'd be the grand Pooh Bah
if it weren't for my legs like arm-like levers, and I have a horn like a tubahh.

I am more gall than god—is what the high gods say in communion.

Still, I'm telling this story. And I'll be the most unreliable narrator in all directions
from a center or point of reference around here. And I give all the directions.
When I say "around here,"

you say:

the earth's motion around its axis or *only a few advisors around the party leavers*
understood their motives or . . . or: 23 *in the vicinity of: the country around Boston* . . .

which is in and around where this story happens to you believers—
You, Me, Who & We

Around the clock. So:

Do not turn round
or come round . . . belatedly

—as when Spring rolls around again . . .
like an excuse.

Feck

Others, as They Appear

The God Twins, **Lord and Lady Lord**: More god-flies than gods. Mannions. One bright, one dim. Connivers. A slight whiff of onion hangs over. He is god of chaos and / or whim. She's to become a god of obscurity and lesser invertebrates. See oblivion.

Con macConghaile: Eleventh century West of Ireland deity descended from seals—the milk of which seals, sucked, occasionally results in a calling or a call, e.g., *please call off your dog*; *I can call spirits from the vastie deepe*; and *His parents named him Little Con but the boys called him Jim*. . . . (It's possible it's "descended from eels.")

Dick Conneely: A mid-level coastal deity descended from the macConghailes—cannot call up spirits or call off dogs. Perpetually calls in sick and okay. He's come to America (New Ireland) by way of the sea rowing a wherry with a whisk.

The Mannions—of the West (of Ireland): Pests. A rival sept of inland gods perpetually warring with coastal gods and favoring highly protective tariffs.

The Lords of the Low Grasses: Those few snakes extant before snakes are thrown out of Ireland by the cold. The Irish king snake the only remainder.

The Sisters of Charity of Halifax: A bad batch sent to Boston in the early 1950's.

A Rogue Nun: Her red hair cow-licking out from under her cowl seems a striptease to a boy at St. Margaret's School. It is as if Norway calves from Sweden with a sound expressing astonishment. Cowl for wimple for the internal rhyme. It's that simple.

You, Me, Who & We: The collective listener speaker narrator, all unreliable, confused, troubled by odd or capricious notions.

Mister I. Imagination: The title character from a children's television series of the 1950's. He conducts children on train trips to Imagination Land.

Aunt Snookie: Author's aunt; a metaphorical sister of ("The Precious Girl Walks Down the Narrow Street" girlie girl). Her admonishment to *be cahf-ful* is not forgotten.

The O'Malleys: A sea-faring sept controlling the Irish Seas, smugglers, pirates, rapparees. Ruled two territories—the Owles of O'Maille in County Mayo, Connacht, in the West of Ireland. They now take their tea with milk and sugar and in cups the size of coracles. See Imagination and Snookie.

Septs: "Septs are multitudes of the ſame name, and pretended family or lineage in Ireland, ſo called." *Blount's Glossographia*, second edition, London, 1661.

The God of Luck: That god. The coin-flipper (also see **Lord** for like behavior).

Mikey Mulkerrin: A stand-in for the butcher's helper. He flutters at our window like a kitchen moth. He is our hero . . . *in the many multitudes of zero* . . . not our savior!

The Archangel: Failed altar boy. See Mikey Mulkerrin (one and the same).

Irish Latin Holders: Those fervent Irish Catholics in America devoted to their priests.

Mikey's Ma and Da: Died at sea. See reference in "Moon / Moth" herein.

Tinni, King of Connacht, Son of macConri: In the Ulster Cycle of Irish Mythology, Tinni was king until replaced by the fair-haired wolf queen, Maeve. He regained a share of the throne when he became Maeve's lover. In a thousand years, macConri translated to King.

The Butcher: An apprentice; a force in opposition to Mikey.

Nula Gannon: Dick Conneely's henchwoman; barkeep. A facilitator. A godling with magic.

Sister Nursey Mannion: Legendary Southie battle captain and midwife. Local mythology has it that she had the power to transport Souls. Once worked at the old Carney Hospital. Dismissed from her religious order under (a cloud?) clouded circumstance(s).

Casper's: A South Boston Funeral Parlor.

Mikey's Mum: See his Ma and Da.

The Precious Girl Walking Down the Voluptuous Street: Mysterious wife / mother type.

The Butcher's Helper: A job once held by author's father. And is not the butcher who's the aforementioned apprentice. Though, perhaps they were acquainted figuratively—not literally.

FECK

Why hop ye so, ye high hills? This is God's hill, in the which it pleaseth him to dwell: yea, the Lord will abide in it forever.

from *The Book of Common Prayer,* Psalm 68

Wherein:

Neighborhood gods present as naïve pests associated with small-minded men and which gods hold to the illusion of the divinely complex. They nest as one in the ordinary latrine. And have less power than one green-headed fly has over another. Aether. Rotty flows. Blood. Nuns burning the charity out of children, etc.

Should there be a beginning or ending that differs . . .?

Are we bespoke by the gods . . .?

Bad Latin

. . . and we have come to the altar of God . . .

        The god twins believe
they double everything,

yet simply share a common plane of atoms
which has them two-dimensional

and second-guessing. We natural-borns
are wiser by twice—

only lose our wisdom
as we inquire.

        This is how it begins:
before Aramaic.

        Before skins. Before
womb rhymes tomb.

        Before there are different kinds of smart.

        Children discover this in their year eight.

        Why wait?
        Though when midwives hibernate

souls for later,
        they think that's smart—

though it's not.
                        Nor is this—when

one is eleven—say, ten—
old for a child, still

before the body's clock's
placed in its sepulcher,

there's the moment
each child imagines

it's wiser than it's ever been,
        imagines a new Old and a new New Testament.

Feck, a God

Holds the mountain on the moon of an arse—
is what gods high and low whisper behind his back.

It's a small hallowed hill is left to him by his Da,
Con macConghaile, descended from seals
or is it a sept of indolent sea lions died off

before gods abandoned the sea—misaligned
themselves with land creatures, birds,
and small-minded men?

It is a wonder how gods keep
their own wet, fetid lives—to say nothing
of how they keep their god wives when

these gods—everywhere and indiscreet—
are a low pestilence since the laws of the universe
constricted the airs and gases to a core of chem-
compounds common such that both god and gas
nest as one in the ordinary latrine.

And still, we—they, hold to the illusion of the divinely complex.

And in all systems solar, there is a rise and a fall,
with skeletal moons scattered like pebbles holding
the interest of seekers looking up at the skies—

at the mystery.

In the Before & Far-out, Feck, by happenchance,
captures the first bolt of thunder drummed out of atmosphere,
entwined with the first strike of light bolt-faulted
to the earth's first mud. By virtue of this scepter
and the holding of the holy hill by inheritance—

this holy hill, with all its shock-ed memory
for *ever was ever will be*'s—

by virtue of these banalities, Feck has
the high office of our world's Supreme Being just as Fergus Wry-
mouth once held all Ireland in fealty when he dug
his boots into the Hill of Tara, and, despite
his protestations to the contrary, shook
fearfully in those clotty leathers.

And so it is that Hierarchicals
have as much well-held power amongst
their peers as might one green-headed fly
have over another, their swarm teasing
a horse's eye imagining
they have the beast

when it's the fecking horse
has *them* occupied, busy
at the feast of eyes and neighs—

the fool god-flies disremembering
any nature of their own,
significant.

Hierarchicals

It is by their base nature that gods are greenhorns—
naïve pests better at mobbing than mobbing up—
or tweaking the yellow to green plumage
of a large finch or confusing a damselfly.

There is a set of twins, boy and girl—
if gods may be sexed, who came after the failed
almighties. After the seal-boy—the aquanaut, Dick Conneely,
after his estranged uncles fell, and after his great-nephew
is deposed by the Mannions, and long after

the descent of the Lords of the Low Grasses—
more salamander than snake, small-mouthed,
mute and segmented as centipedes, known only
for depressing the nameless

grasses as they slithered toward the Hill where,
until finally deposed by a dry storm,
they run our magnificent miniverse
for mindless millennia.

Deposed by a storm which births
the twins' antecedents (so a history oral has it),
those two bits who are never much to look at—or see
for their blend-all pallor (and blind to themselves, too),

those hairless infant minutia are named godlings
of a sort and rendered holy, rather than curiosities,
until such time as there's a genesis

of a sense of transient ethereal nonsense findings

made by family about family and place,
and who is who relative to nuance,
and the various colorations appearing,
it seems, out of nowhere, yet relative to

the fuzzy goings-on in the heavens

that were the Hill and its proximities.

Came then the aether and the ichor.

(Six Plain Colourless Faces) See Next Poem about (A)Ether & Ethereal Fluids

By way of preemptive explanation:

Removed and laid flat, your skin occupies about twenty square feet of . . .
territory. The corners are plain and without colour. So, is a face (1) with skin
-lesions, dull and gray, one of the six plain? Or marked? And is six the smallest . . .
perfect natural number—if any of six (prism) faces of ____ show striations?

Is water one face (2) boiling at part of four right angles? Is light a face (3) lustrous
as in large, lusterless eyes? Is the face (4) of adamantine, laid flat, "unbreakable,"
or is it diamond-like with six facets? Are all face colours set to "flat"? And if so,
if a cookie is laid flat, face up, and split into two pieces, then what?

Plain City, Utah, is one of the faces (5). It is pale brassy yellow. But on gray days
it is so pale it looks sickly.

Pearly and Pearly White is another less definite colourless metallic face (6). Six
plain colourful faeces.

All clear here?

(7) As to what kind of a creation story this is—see Muddle.

Aether

Comes in a cup.

And ichor, before it's the rotty flow from a wound
runs, as blood might, in the veins of gods

—that any god might sup
from the wound of a brother.

But not in the beginning:

If there ever is such a thing as begin.

If ever there is a moment of pre-house-broke.

If ever there is a time of not.

If ever there is.   Or are we bespoke
by the gods or

by the sheer will of a self? And why is it

beginnings appear to appear in sets of six—six plain
faces which make a sort of hexahedron?

And will there ever again be a timely timeless time
without these six plain colourless faces—

or a deity represented by a fetish?

Or is it that—at any given time, a prompt might be
one to three

and promises? Or similar but not exactly the same
as the cup of ether served up

with a two-and-a-half-year old's
tonsillectomy

as if it were a psalm.

    Now, *that* was a beginning!

* * *

    Ether comes in a cup. Drink it all at once.

    This long before the Sisters of Charity of Halifax
have their convent fire. Which fire

and an obscure hand-me-down collective memory
of it, which is passed to novitiates—burns the charity

out of generations of them except for one

—orange hair nicking from under her wimple
on the convent stairwell—she calls a boy

Sunshine—and that lasts well past a half-life
of sacraments, hapless.

    All this to say

        the gods say what . . .

. . . We Want Them to Say

Or is it a misunderstanding of what's generally
misunderstood—or tossed away?

And could there be a beginning or an ending differs
from that one what's settled upon at St. Margaret's School

in the year of our lord and lady, 1949, when a rogue
nun tells the origin story of the twins, fingers

crossed—twisting behind her back—

to the seven-year-olds
—who will believe anything.

Some tellings leave a tell.

The physicists can go to hell.

THE CREATION
(NOT TO BE CONFUSED BY . . .)

Wherein:

There were prizes once . . . and more riddles unsolvable—and mindless games. This book is the handbook of such. Say anguish. Religiosity flickers. How is it we tell a spell has been broken? Or traverse a Multiverse with . . . blue fragrant gum resin seeping. . . . And who are we to say how bitter curses are broken? Keeping in mind that forgiveness has an odor older than the Pleistocene . . . and where, if anywhere, is the place where shame pudding might be absolved, etc.

God loves a cheerful giver. It says so in the book. . . .
We vibrate in our skins . . .

It's Just a Threnody Game

not a song of lamentation

There were prizes, once, for using the finest
tomato products you ever tasted. But

that's over. Now it's guessing games
and teasers.

Who knows a game of fours without bowls or boats?

(It's not easy to be told to play precious with words.
Not easy to know the importance of roughage—not easy
to distinguish among the ruffage of language
and the rough edges of languish.)

Who knows a game of fives without walls or balls?

Anybody a player?

Yet it seems a lot of things or stuff seem(s) easy
if there's a handbook—and this book is a handbook,
though why is it handbook examples are harder?
For example:

They don't have no home. It was so noisy
I couldn't hardly hear myself think. We never do nothing
but talk about the weather.

We cannot afford to stand by and do nothing about this.
This is the handbook. Say anguish.

Who knows of a game of sixes and sevens without a state
of confusion or
disarray. . .?

Or it ends with a race of eight-oared boats.

Begin.
With a prayer.

Oyster Beliefs

A surprise Easter sunrise sees religiosity flickering.
It's soon significant dark mass time—
High-Church stuff slow to change.

For every two new saints, we lose
a favorite. There's none now

for losers. Silence is not there to signify.

Nuns no longer creep down the stairs.

And when we wonder why we wonder or if
a sign is not a signal, how is it we tell

whether there's a spell
to be broken—or is this stuff small

in the highly competitive industry
of settled dogma and porcelain

figurines handed down
contemptuously?

Who

is it says so?

Who slings a filched gospel, who
sabbaths with a leaf blower going

like a carillon?

And when the hard questions are half-cocked

and Easter comes a-rising,

who is it's survived by the many
devoted . . .

who by the lame?

Muddle

OK. Let's get over the universe we've never been under
and huddle.

As you know, it has a lining which is cotton or
one of the polys. Let's scissor it asunder as if

we are an old mariner from Gloucester
golloping his scallops and peeing in his boot.

Now what if what we've cut scars?

We've all broken promises,
know that forgiveness has an odor
older than the Pleistocene.

And, yes, it will take a human wedge
like a pie slice to drive into
that Wedgwood potty you
have for a thick skull.

You're past the easy way
and beyond the time of dreams.

You've no slick way in or out;
there's no more bullshit from minor prophets—

no poets' blood to spill.

So let's walk up to these whatever universettes,

to their never before—

all drill sergeant and pretending . . .

Little Bang Chaos

Don't bother to fear the nightmare wherein

there's a perpetual and timeless season when
we're universally vulnerable to the whims and
fancies of the divine—a time when kindred gods

pluck seed from each's peaches, and plums too,
succumb—which might make Latin's Hierarchies
simpler than rice pudding, yet your silly sins

of the mouth still digest the context of must-do ritual
or slang for something impolite as in *nice pud-*
endum. Whew!

(Which is the first place where shame pudding
would be absolved.)

Keep at it. Push back what stills. Cut away
all the hair that sticks out; make a short burst—

do not take a full breath; *she plumb forgot* . . . or
in lieu of one, a pair of bones forming . . .

All of this is uncomfortable but
none of this is unnatural, and its corrugate—

its corollary—contracting into wrinkles
and whim is like a holiday in the sun—

and not just the romance novel and cancer
-preventing hat keeping cancer off

like a crow keeps off the crow
from its kill, and is like—or not quite like
but similar, say, as what rushes in crushes—or a
feast commemorating the institution of the Eucharist.

Or that time she said, “you should use another term for maim.”

Not as in: *the constant stricture of the nuns . . .*

but as in Scripture—*the Holy Scripture, for Christ’s sake,*

eat of this!

Space-Time Cutlets

Today, in a manner of speaking,
is just another relaxing laundry day—

another distributed source of power
bursting in space-time

already junked up

with surly dark matter in the heaven—
but on the earth, we're thinking we're okay

with things & anti-things being our power source,
since, to us, those are never spent or gone

to where stuff is sent when it rhymes
with worn out or torn from or theatrical;

because we know, in time, it'll
be symmetrical or off but a little,

so, then (and wrongly), to us it's okay
the way some see a point

standing on one end or its other
or, in lieu, say, see sideways, a

wave waving in the aether.
And remember, it's not as if you'd be

passed by, or it's too mathematical,
or we *are* or we *were*   or we always will be . . .

The Enormous

God loves a cheerful giver. It says so in the book . . .

Giving the right answer is a gift. One we have come to expect.

It would be a mammoth achievement—as in understanding
the four enormous families within which are organized

the groups flipping and rotating. Better keep a steady hand.
Better keep your conversations symmetrical and moving.

Whether or not it's about weather, one way or another, dark
one-dimensional matter-filled weather-like conversation

smothers answers. *Be cahf-ful!* says Aunt Snookie.

And beware the dying off of mathematicians:

In their game of threes, the cube has three pairs of
opposite faces, etc.—and its universe turn, turn, turns.

And handbook examples
are harder.

Is there a baptismal font filled for wish and wash?
Somewhere, is there some wishy-washy liqueur

evaporating on the brow of the lip of
the youngster expected to pick up their pieces? And—

Do not paint the faces; the math will go bad.

And remember, a universe represented by a cube has eight
corners represented by an aforementioned eight-oared boat.

Boats keep cubey things believing they are safe *in utero*.

Also—in the game of eights, there are eight corners. Twelve edges.

It is easier now that the handbook explains—but here's a question:

The infinite lie—is there an answer formulating

in the many multitudes of zero?

A Game of Fives . . .

And count.

A hospice midwife welcomes to her home a ghost—
a man just died in her care who, imagining
he belongs with whomever loved him last,
uses up all there is of his last legs.

To follow his latest love, is how he tells it.

Two. We have lost a favorite. Not a daughter
or a son or anyone we care about. Someone
we know in passing who knew the ancient
past from memory, the dregs

of which were kept in the reaches of his fridge,
found after a plug is pulled like a loose tooth—
he who was or is a boy of eleven—or ten when,

three, he's already forgotten a tooth god
and the stumps of tree gods petrified.

Three gods he is told there are, three of
three—and equal. The yew and the oak
no greater than the soft, yellow pine
he found it difficult to believe in—
its wood impressed by a thumbnail.

Four then, if one counts the god of teeth
and the endings

of nerves—and pain, the god of pain,
and its phantom. That god. Those multiples of god.

No need here for missionaries.

Five.

FIVE

. . . I cannot find in all the Bible, the name archangel but twice . . . And as for archangels, as if there were more than one, or many, the very name itself implies that it is an error. For archangel signifies the first . . . the question is, who is this archangel?

–from *The Poor Man's Concordance*, 1828

Wherein:

Conflict. Dick Conneely cedes his Irish kingdom to mice. . . . He pisses on his boots, power pooling at his feet; imagines a future in America. Frog Pond, Boston Common—angels bathe here. Mikey Mulkerrin arrives. He is out of St. Mary's Infant Asylum. Discovered by Lord and Lady, they imagine him their Archangel—who will lead the locals to their sway. Origin story of the twin gods encapsulated using references to an 18th century text on midwifery. Conneely arrives in America and is quick to foretell his own demise. The Archangel matures. Lord and Lady Lord conspire. Feck, a Supreme Being, intercedes (at a distance) to bring order. A Watch & Ward Society is formed—the intent is to encourage memory loss and slow momentum. And too, a reminder:

Twins, divine, are unheard of—except in books of gods.

Down the Hill and Under

It's a costly day at the Hill.
Dick Conneely's tumbled down
having ceded his kingdom to mice

and the Mannion twins of the West, as they are known
in the hereabouts. They've pulled down the excess skin
is how they put it. One fat god to two thin gods, twice
the drudge of time it takes for third place

and obsolete—

which is how old Dick's seen by these twin gods
running the fields and moors as if there is no more
there than stubbed grass and rock to lord over.

Conneely, his bad half balancing on his war stick,
falls toward the bottom of the world. He stops to piss—
imagines he'll beat the Mannions to death
with this blackthorn . . .

Is how he sees it—his power pooling at his feet
as he misses a rock he pisses at, finds a ditch to wet
which respite moment has him over another hill—

imagining the future lineage of *acequias* watering
the southwest of America—remembering a succession

of roadway ditches in mid-twentieth-century California—
before there is an America.

. . . Big Bajada. Union. Bula. Tapo. Hillock. Wide Ditch.
Tex Wash. Larry Ditch. Desert Creek. Desert Well. Airport
Ditch. Coxcomb. Quartz. Ghost. Rollie Ditch. Pallen
Ditch. Meta Ditch. Oban Ditch. Copa. Aztec. Sultro
Ditch. Arantola Ditch. Wiley's Well. Mud Ditch. Arco
Ditch. Esso Ditch. Beehive Ditch. Acari Ditch. Rubble

Ditch. Alta Ditch. Rannell's Drain. Pallo Wallo Ditch.
McCoy Wash. Gale Ditch. Teed Ditch. Calada Ditch.
Walla Ditch. Mud Ditch . . .

10,000 Videos. Please ask about Colorado River . . .

Yes. America. And the White Star Line
out of Queenstown—when his time repeats.

And long after the reign of the sea gods—
the sea given the O'Malleys by Himself.

Long after the faction fights and tenants ruined by lessors.

Then, when the midwives and the archangel are his—

by the god of luck, he'll rule in the New World.

Ablutions

Frog Pond. Boston Common.
Angels bathe here. Where else
are they to bathe?

All orders of them, high to low,
new and glorious, the faded ones
in their pastel.

Who comes here
who sees them?
None of you.

And who would believe
if children do?
Not you.

Who amongst the believers believe
enough to see their failing grace rinsed
from the tatter wings they keep in tatters?

Who amongst the believers
forgives their sins, forgives
their being at the waters

cleansing themselves as if
they were at a blood
spot, weeping?

Look—at the shallow by the pond's lip.

There's little Mikey Mulkerrin wetting his cochinealed wings.

One of Them Goes Like This

Flight of the Archangel Mulkerrin, Dorchester, 1899

Each day, it is—and seems it forever is

just another laundry day at St. Mary's Infant Asylum
with its fresh supply of crust-eyed babies paired
in cubbies as if they're twins waiting for the nipples
of a wet nurse god. Once weaned, they're dry
nursed with the tailings of some common thing
or the scree of whatever fish head porridge,
is at process at Mary's, which are the makings
of what's nowadays branded:
Saint Mary's Famous Baby Chowder.

It's also home to a first baby powder—
a form of dry scalp, untended till it is swept.

No midwifery here. No archangels kept.

There is some Latin at the coving over the front doors says:
Be Quick and Quickly Multiply, etc.

Might it be this dictum keeps the hostel busy
with the poorest of the Irish Latin holders—
and Boston seeming but a pit of stuporous
gravidity to the asylum's watchers who see
each birth as an expulsion?

There are feral grasses at the rear gates
on Everett Ave wherein a spat of feral children
nest till there's a rub of reverse transubstantiation—

or devolution goes unnoticed by all but one
who lies still till his toes root to the gray compost
holding loose particles of our Earth unbound.

Until he is bound into the new morning then
pushes himself loose, crawls.

* * *

And the Lord mistook what Lady Lord said:

Heard: *One amongst you is one of them*
who plays this game of fours.

And our Lady says, *incorrect*:
game on *all* fours—as in
whomever crawls off

is our archangel.

Glyph / Glitch

see Smellie's *A Treatise on the Theory and Practice of Midwifery,* London, 1751

Some see it as a wish.
Some see it as a sin.
She sees it as a child.

He sees it as a fish.
This is how twins begin
in the wild

imagination of a careless
mother god
wanton god . . . see

BOOK III CHAP. V.

Of Twins.

Twins are ſuppoſed to be the effect
of a double conception in one coition,
when two or more Ova are impregnated with
as many animicula; which deſcending from
the Ovarian, through the Fallopian tube, into . . .

a somehow familiar and friendly abyss but
not in this example wherein nothing's rightly
doubled but . . . see

SECT. II

Of Monsters.   where

. . . No certain rules can be laid down in theſe
caſes, which ſeldom happen, and therefore a
great deal muſt be left to the judgement and
ſagacity of the operator . . .

Hence and hereafter, the art of midwifery is
transmogrified, and wrongly, to a holy order
jurisdicted by some god of wrong—gifting

power as if it were a gift, and hereafter and hence,
bent midwives twist arms and legs, unstrangle what beast
it is a god might birth in birthing havoc and disorder . . .

Who First

And does it matter
when there are so many made-up
porridge god and origin stories to lose
track of where

some see it as chowder?
Or some see it as a glitch

which means *who first*
might just be petty religiosity (or pettifoggery)

as in which of the twin gods counts for more

than the other—the girl one called Lady Lord
being more *here* than that one

who's hopelessly atmospherical?

And neither or both with or without genitalia for an easy distinction made and unmade so that complex may be seen simply as a mutilation easily accepted

or denied as with the missing pistils and stamens of crushed flowers.

And their edicts as if out of a book of primitive tells
believable because it's read by children beginning

pubescence before eleven—perhaps ten, who we imagine
have imaginations rarified—wherein all gods' images

are in slick two-dimensional realms common
amongst the adolescent, shorter, lesser

simpler gods of skim or folly, for example.
But unheard of in the Hierarchy—if you can believe that.

Not imagined on a flat plane where convention is, and

complex gods rule side-by-side and adjacent.

And nothing came in pairs at the top.

Twins, divine, were unheard of—

except in books of gods.

Provocative Mania

Dick's late to the Americas.

Whenever it's time for him to leave—
and again and again—repeating for millennia,
he distracts himself, keeps from falling forward
by telling stories to his grandchildren,
most of which stories speak to a dying
into or out of Irish, or the absence
of a connection to
an historical past that is peripheral to now.

Or he reads to them from the lucky penny scriptures,
or tells the innocents that it's never smart to do anything
by cycles of moons or under the influence
of mildly intoxicating preparations of leaves and
flowering tops of any flora what so ever.

Or how not to go benthic at the bottoms
of the holy waters—
the intent is a sudden and quickly done bracing swim
much as done in winter out of the L Street bathhouse.

He mentions, too, the need for underpinnings
and a name change kit.

Much too much for most of them to swallow,
he belatedly realizes—and as it is with
birds drunk on pyracantha berries,
and the tweaked swallows of the New World
modified such they are unable to patch mud nests . . .
and water dogs drunk on fermented figs
sobered on doses of black tea dry bread, etc. So it is

with the god, Conneely, belatedly seeing himself drunk
on a nameless disquietude having to do with displacement
and abandonment, and thereafter concludes he speaks nothing
to his descendants but air and aerologies.

And this, to him who is a god, is near overwhelming until—
there is a self-diagnosis mildly epigrammatick
which appears, stills him. Thinks this:

It is ending—that great crimp of time which is mine.

Attend to its remainders or its corrugates in the time-
space place wherein / if—there's a buckling—much
like the creping of old skin some call crinkles.

Which puts him with a vertiginous sense of
bending out of his nebulous fleshy parts.

Until, one day, awakening, and high on life—
so to speak, he assembles his few belongings
into a tidy kit, imagines himself in steerage
on the White Star's *S.S. Baltic* before it's built—

and, disappointing as it is for all of you who await,
then has a last-minute excuse which has him
working the docks in Queenstown till
thereabouts 1897 or 1898.

Leaves then, arrives late.

Advantage, god twins.

Moon / Moth

Mikey flutters like a kitchen moth at your window.

He is arrived while Feck sleeps; the new kingdom
of the New World nursed by midwives of the court of Lady Lord
who jurisdicts while Lord weeps over the spilt and spoilt.

The twins have little baby faces like the moons of Gold
Street between Fourth and Fifth—or similar but not
the same as the Firth of Forth's eclipsing

lesser bodies of water in the mind of a lesser king reigning
over the midlands, spritzing piss on rooftops to be mean-
spirited. Spirited, yes, spirited—as if shunted off

the Island with a broom; swept into the Atlantic—a boat
with no oars was how Mikey's Ma and Da drink the sea

in a death ship guised as a steamer disguised

as a vessel leaving home for oblivion.

And they were swept away because they are parables
for loss then lost, is how he is found at St. Mary's Asylum
for bed-wetters and the eternally anxious.

And there is a constant remnant of altar boy's Latin
ringing his head's bell telling of new loyalties—
the great king Tinni, King of Connacht, son of macConri—

and all of the least gods and kings are unmoored
in the mind of Mikey now that the twins have swiped
his history—made their past his past.

The Hill

After her swim, Lady emerges from the reservoir on Dorchester Heights, walks down Telegraph Street to St. Augustine's Church on Dot Ave.

Conneely waits at the hill till he hears the door of the church open and close. Then he drains the reservoir for good.

Lady burns candles for the lost souls she's lost. At the altar she kneels, pretends to pray; upon leaving, she empties the poor box. Bells peal.

Conneely's busy at annoying the twins for three years
before it's decided something's to be done to him—that is,
until *she* decides—Lord not deciding on any one thing over
another except by coin flip—which hasn't gone unnoticed
by parishioners and hierarchicals.

Plain angels in the neighborhood are growing unnoticed
into their adolescence. Some are getting work permits,
will soon begin attending you and yours—as will
the new midwives blooming at untended graves
like Russian thistle.

And all your babies born *do* seem allergic.
There is a Cavanaugh has a nervous sneeze.

It is a time of turmoil for the mindful, and wounds
appearing at the wrist.

There are too many of the chosen few. And the gods—
they are stepping over one another like penned sheep.

So, with the anonymous backing of a supreme being,
a Watch & Ward Society is formed.

Some see this as an attempt at time stilled for catch-up.
It is more for memory loss and momentum slowed.

Images are broken to blue glass shards. Myths are booked
and cyphered. Belief systems spread virally to a randy

new awareness like a haul of walrus in song
or a plague of good gone wrong.

The twins, well into early adulthood, plot against
the scourge which is Conneely.

A corruption of lesser angels (six or seven)
is mustered to signal the end of his remnants

of Eminence—to deal with the confusion
and disarray that is Dick Conneely

who is suddenly called away
on matters of family—or so he says.

WATCH & WARD

Wherein:

Confusion. Lord is appointed bother god over a newly formed Watch & Ward Society. Feckless gods scheme. Religiosity resurrects. See the two twining stories of Mikey and the Butcher. Conneely returns and retakes the Hill. Mikey interns amongst the fallen angels.

. . . You have to choose a cut as part of the ritual . . .

Send God

By the gods—or some such things as those,
is how this came and went, or so the story goes—

about the odd business at the once abandoned
Fire House on East Eighth, which house seems—
to our Lord—to be of another era, the stones appearing
much the same, if not the very same, as those of a folly
at Phillips Manor—those Phillips of Ickford in the County
of Bucks, that estimable family known for their
advocacy of midwifery in England's colonies.

This small confusion is unsettling to Lord, who,
for a moment, feels in an awkward space and time,
and then, quickly, he conjures an astral venue
without architecture, wherein his moments are
ably spent fussing over the faces of coins—
ought they be up, or ought they be down.

And, as it's near eventide, there's his
fuss over a waste of candlewick on light.

And he is the first to put the match
of womb and tomb to bed at night.

It's he is named bother god to this society,
the Charter of the Watch & Ward's to him,

who is god of chaos and / or whim.

It's he imagined first, the frigid L Street swim.

When you say godsend, they send him.

Watch & Ward Society, South Boston Chapter

Think of it as a corruption by the executive binary.

Believe ossuary not estuary.
Feel a feeling of usefulness
preceding a period of decline.

Halve that, then think gods at play. Lady in recline
letting Lord have his way recruiting Watch & Warders

while she's imagining the locals as a second growth forest ripe.

Lord misinterpreting and misapplying the Ten Commandments . . .

Until she finally must dissuade him from a notion that murdering
in a past life is a disqualifier to membership except as an auxiliary.

Lady says it's not a question put to parishioners, many of whom might
commit such crimes in dreams and feel guilt over what's dreamt—

while she knows there's no crime if it's a lying dream—

the most common kind of dream, and especially if,
within the dream, one is found guilty

and is punished—though there never seems to her,
to be a full and just reckoning in dreams of any kind,
for one's past lies—which has her rethinking capital
death and metempsychoses.

All of which is a distraction. She reminds herself
before reminding Lord, that, if a "why" question is posed,
he is to tell an inductee-to-be that it's likely about
a bad mattress.

Or dodge the answer. Membership is a ruse.

It's more a round-up of the locals
meant to seem a benevolent gather
for the common good

when it's really a malevolent sweep
meant to net an archangel.

You Know Who You Are

Those of you descendant from first night inductees
at Watch & Ward No. 1.

That evening:

To aggravate and dishearten, the hierarchy brings a skep
of summer horse flies which sets like a cake on an altar-
like rectory table salvaged from a diminished realm of
Protestantism.

There are midwives in a makeshift crying room flush
with blue babies waiting to revitalize. And Sister Nursey
Mannion, the reformed convent runner, is here, and rings
a recess bell for order.

She works a clapper to signal signals, and parishioners
seem to know them, as if they'd been to clapper signal school.

Is it in their blood?

And some wish up their hacking cough as an excuse to leave—
but have a fear of using it and stay.

And as they seem easy kneelers, it seems, too,
that they've attended
kneeling school.

Would you all please rise and undo the Sign of the Cross backwards . . .

asks the old convent runner, lifting the lid on the lies.

Mikey

If Mikey were to tell the story, it's him in a room with a lamb.

He is hung by block and tackle from a ceiling timber.
His body is inked for retail cuts or wholesale cuts
—he doesn't know the difference. The meaning
of marks on meat is for the butcher to know.

The lamb wanders the room bleating.

The butcher has a case of abattoir nerves.
This task is a first for him. His knives have
dank gray hands and pink cheeks as do
the lamb, Mikey, and himself.

If the butcher tells the story, he—

an apprentice—winches the butchered lamb closer to Mikey
so that he may choose . . .

a latter part of a period of time. The shank

is what Mikey's thinking—when the butcher might
think loin chops, but says:

You have to choose a cut as part of the ritual . . .

sacrifice, Mikey says, finishing the boy's words
aloud, as he looks up and smiles, and then thinks:

The story's contrived ending is a . . . knife

Or the butcher is not that nervous and he winches
Mikey over to the lamb so that *she* can choose.

Either way, either story, you lose if you believe

Mikey dies here before he saves your world.

or

Either way, either story, you choose to believe
Mikey loses here before he saves the world.

Worst Angels

They've journeyed,

not fallen
from grace or from the good
grace of the enumerated gods—

those nameless unnumbered
we imagine slinking over
the peninsula looking for
a hole
to crawl in,

worming toward
the great cavity of our viscus
organs to home, imbedding
like an earwig into
the soul's intestine

where they are abed
        but not asleep.

        Those weak-ass gods.
        Those badass angels.

        Those figments: the noises in the attic
were just _____ of his imagination.

        Nevertheless and because and despite their being an army of the mind—

        it's Mikey is their theater of war.

The White Sea

In a grandmother's great teacup,
a reservoir of gray tea,
Hood's milk, and spooned
white-sharp granules
are the fractal
boundary
to your imaginary
peninsula,   I mean to say

when they come for you
as might their demons—
out of Pleasure Bay—
retreat to the Heights.
Conneely's returned
and has put the kettle on.

He's made a memory
of the mist of the dead
reservoir
as one might make tea—
and takes the Hill
as his own.

And, no, they've not yet peeled away
the scare of wallpaper from the bedroom
you shared as a frightened child, though
the room is long gone. Be wary
before you allow to feel safer—
or don't till

the one day, the willing gods
will the knives out of butter—

or move priests out of diocese.

But that's not anything to do with you.

Fractal

Lager. Froth. Fraternal
neighborhood tavern HQ
harboring shame-shouldered
men—stoic cabbies and bunged-
up longshoremen, arses
and bollocks aroost on
hard wooden stools
screaking over the hard wet
wooden floor with every arm-wave—

or what jerk-legged startle
has them into a neighbor's face
when suddenly spoken to—
brought back amongst
the living an instant
before a quick retreat—

these glorious be-lied-to men.

And here interns Mikey with a broom,
released, he believes, by the redeemer
twins, one of whom has the patience
of a coven of nuns anticipating
the sins of schoolchildren.

He's not forgotten—or shelved
amongst the countless orders of fallen angels

at Conneely's Den.

The Watered Down

Gods hinder perpetually,
not bound to either order or to chaos.

But to both. *It all evens out* is what's decided
at the gatherbabble of the High and Mighties,

by the god twins and Conneely's barkeep, Nula Gannon—
his henchwoman, as good a cut and carver

as any butcher or bargain-maker—

a hard bargain made having bartered for her son's life
and won him an hour more on the killing field.

And later, hustling Lord at *Find-the-Lady*
till he owed her another life

which she would hold over him till long after
they buried her out of Casper's.

It was Nula nicked the archangel—
and that hour her son got

as his last at the great faction
fight on the Heights

the night Conneely
took the ground—

and she became immortal—
for all practical purposes,

having nothing more to lose.

A NATURAL SCENE

Wherein:

The low gods express their incomprehensible worldview. They regroup. Mikey, the archangel in flux, is discovering his powers. High gods disappointed in the twin gods' choice of archangel. Lord and Lady withdraw. Mikey withdraws inward. Who knows him—who keeps his hours? Nula bargains with Conneely to keep Mikey safe. What next for Mikey? The archangel cometh.

. . . let me explain in words you will understand . . .

Scary Wallpaper Dream

Even gods—immortal, will sleep poorly, made
insomniatic in the imaginings of their creators—

sleep-deprived aboriginals

searching the night sky imagining
the never ending.

Tonight, her rotations make of her a finite soup.

Lady Lord, restless in her bed, is dreaming
a handbook's boats are eight Welsh coracles—

each leathered boat with an oar and an oracle
racing to a vanishing point vanishing at one of eight

wooly mammoths, for a handbook example.

She doesn't dream as you do—
does not see the natural

scene clearly—sees lonely

with a worm's eye view—has you

incomprehensible.

If any of these marbles are yours, let me know.
Most of the potatoes are already gone.
If any of this cake is yours, let me know.
Most of the evening is already gone . . .

And unless she wakes composed—a god dies here

shapeless.

As could you in any sleep's whisty circumstance

if not gifted the daily startle

of a feckless body's

clock   at high alarm.

Reconnoiter

Even we are immortals.

It says so in the *Book of Saves*.

The Watch & Warders still fuss and muster—hapless.

Nula's barroom is the new Cathedral—

her backroom card room pressed to the jambs

with angels—the eight kinds less

the archangel, who, having called in sick and okay, is hovering,

with his lush red wings,

over the old graves

for the practice.

Winged

He hasn't a means of measuring, or a sense for scale.
He wonders about his feather architecture—

whether he's got the wingspan of the Great Albatross
or of the greater dragonfly—or of a kitchen moth—

or whichever fly or flit is winged such that when
hovering over the Hill, anonymous,

without the flourish of a provenance
or an origin story—
why is it that he arrives flapping

and whispering a palest of hallelujahs
at his own small annunciation?

* * *

Yet the High gods see:

It's as if Lady went to gather an orphan
at the orphan gather, and returned with not
the smallest or the frailest—
not the most vulnerable.

Not the least one—malleable,
but the one most angelical.

Feck wishes he'd let Lord choose
by coin flip

now that Mikey's spread his wings magnificent—
has grown into a guardian.

. . . When the plan was

for him to lead all of Southie to oblivion.

The Archangel, Michael

Quill. Shaft. Vane.
Feather. He
has learned
to swallow
feathers.

Appears
colorless.

Is absent from
the new world of words
and talk

and want.

Holds to the wall
when he walks.

He is divisible by one.

Invisible to you
who

would seem family
if there were blood
shared.

And it is as if
he loves

by virtue
of absence

and
inadvertency.

Yet
he is ever here

and is often called upon
for what seems

is mist.

Oblivion

[L. *Oblivio.*] The act of forgetting, or the state of being forgotten

And Lord has withdrawn to the old country,
which having been seduced by the trick
of a title and small estate on a planar which, in fact, sets on the soft back
of a planarian worm
in the far ferment.

And Lady, nearby, is to become a god
of obscurity and the lesser invertebrates,
having chosen a lost child for a messenger
who has not got the message.

Conneely's powers green the Hill
with switch grass and dandelion.

Nula Gannon, the midwife, mustering
nine orders, calls up the nine orders
of magnitude of the hierarchy of quark
masses, and quickly corrects, stops
at the lowest order of angels

who will serve Michael
who has folded into himself
the wings, unwieldy,

and works awhile
in apprenticeship

until ordinarily employable.

The Lowest Order

Nula's praetorians shadow
Michael while he struggles at the art
of anonymity

despite his preternatural brogue—
that annoying noise that angels
make—which has him amongst us
with the guise of a corruption

of hissing labials
and sharp flats

and gutturals

the pure and the impure
vowel violated.

Shism, shone, bowld,
Cowld bone cowld

Mek'il spakes
with a breath extra
that thickens

into vicious pronunciation

which has him fit in as if he belongs
second-handedly.

Confined Within the Narrow Limits of Acquaintance

One who lies upon the Lurch or upon the Catch;
. . . a kind of Hunting Dog.
Bailey's English Dictionary, 1728

Is what he is. Not known
except amongst those others
who are strange and strangers
to us who claim

he's ours.

But who knows him who
kept his hours

shifting against our own
such we saw him discreetly

as one might see
shells of memory

skittering like the house mouse
into darkness?

There he is now. We

make him up
as needs be—

the archangel cometh.

Things of Any Kind

Will arrange their stuff locally—
in much the way physicists say,
asymmetrically

. . . *let me explain in words you will understand* . . .
and then put parenthetical what is meant for experts.

It is all become the complex crushing rush of exposition
leaving incomprehensible the so-called simplest thing

of that particular kind which knowledge of   we crave
as some bare essential bit

of what we hope might be the smallest
start to a godless answer gives us God—

though nuanced—the way, for example, basaltic
rock no longer means what it used to

aeons ago
when once it meant life's flow.

* * *

And timelessness—it seems so,
so very   there;

foretelling what's not

and in its absence, perhaps

timing *is* everything—
and things of every kind

do arrange their sequences of real

and imagined images locally . .

. . . In Which Case

Foreshadow, foretell—
the mortalists
can go to hell.

An archangel's in the neighborhood
and will go viral again.

As he's done countlessly—
will do again

in other jurisdictions—
in other lives,

veins filled with ichor
and a prehistoric

urge to displace /
disturb

that singularity of the singular
monochromatic once

and once only stub
of born-live-die

doctrinaire which
has us disappear

forget   forgot   forgotten . . .

How silly that seems
in any interim . . .

Annates

(Lat.) First-Fruits out of Spiritual Livings, being the Value of one Year's Profit, anciently paid to the Pope, and now to the King
The New World of Words, 1720

As might a mother, Nula bargains with Conneely
till it's agreed he'll keep Mikey for just one year—
a year wherein Nula will keep him clear
of this god's inclination
to refine Natural Law downward
toward something good
for business, safe
for tourists.

She will not have him ruined.

So it is, as his year begins, Nula revels in blessing baby
oracles bobbing in Pleasure Bay while Mikey first makes
book at the South Boston Yacht Club, takes the towel
concession at the L Street bathhouse, gathers
the nickel *numbers* bets kept beneath statuettes
of the Infant of Prague in three-deckers' foyers
at both ends of Broadway.

And if he is not a prince of the streets, who is?

And when the first fruits of this year are paid,
what's next—a city job or one with the "T"?

And what of his long, fractal life with sojourns
as the missed and mysterious, and the keeping
of quiet as if he were a Carmelite
(and with their subversive taste
for candy) and

the occasional Aegypticum

applied to his cloven

spirit . . .

So, boy-o, she says, *whatever the voices say—wait till I tell you . . .*

Wait—lie hidden and still . . .

Double Infinite

And he's done with his servitude—
at least its arithmetical formalities.

And his ordinary dreams
are common dark nightmares
as if of midwinter or midnight
and remarkable for their
stillness and gloom.

For Mikey, with his anger hails
a kind of doom as if he were
commonly corrupted as is
a faded leaf mid-fall,

or him a gillyflower
turned from a July Flower,

and that serenity first thought as nearly here

is now imagined never here at all.

And it is time, anyway, Nula says,
to get on with the sacrament.

Spread your wings.

Absent an Emblem of Strength or Valor

Having imagined his wings imaginary, he feels fright.

Is thinking *this is me when I am zero*.

In orphaned times, it might be
that a plenary indulgence would help.
Or a wink from a young nun to

a needy child might make
the difference a difference makes.

But now, he's missing the cry-overs
the feral children had when
the feral nuns were sad.

And when he "reasons," it makes him rue
the red and green and bluish particles of light
he long ago discovered behind closed eyelids,

when he imagined disorder evenly distributed
amongst the deserving and the undeserving alike—
as if ever they were or could be alike,
and his feelings blithely set aside—in a blink—
that he might feel a formless momentum

toward whatever vague sentimentality
he might require when wishing up his Mum's life-

boat.

How he longs for her!

How he misses the memory of a god—
and the goblets of red wine waved under
his Sunday nose.

He misses miracles and sacrilege alike.
His is a life in mourn.

Until one day he wobbles toward love
with its conventions of family—

and him imagining him as hero.

OFFERED TO GOD

Wherein:

Restless gods in exile. Mikey falls in love at a distance. Lady Lord plots a return to power. Conneely fades. The archangel saves his life, is mistaken for the Angel of Death. Mikey takes Conneely's power for safekeep. Mikey struggles with identity. He is not a divine messenger. He is a mortal, with his wounds profound . . . What is left to be resolved.

Why do we expect so much of you who were born of us . . . ?

Between Fourth and Fifth

In a neighborhood set on the head of the pin, which
pinned neighborhood a god twin fusses with when
restless while in exile—

the pin pinning a pair of mating damselflies
to Lord's lapel such they seem to Lady
to hold the shape of a heart—

and she says that it is at this moment she notices
the notice Michael takes

of the redhead he sees on Gold—
her observation, made from god-
forsaken galaxies away, reminding
her of her powers—still
extraordinary yet
waning.

And she concocts:

to dose him with dreams—of this narrow girl
walking down the precious street—

and his thoughts of flight re-appear / disappear
amidst this dreaming of the girl—what
philosopher gods would call a dismay
by . . . *The Patterns of Life Dis-assembling*
the Temporal and Spatial Ordinary.

Michael besotted. And Lady Lord
in ascent, feels twice her common
strength slips Lord thc doublc-
headed coin to have them
choose a re-emergence.

Row-a-Dory

Re-appearing, the twins dodge the flat moon,
the far Sphericals—miss the et cetera planeteria
with all their easy ellipticals and essential ascendant
cosmological antics—

which both attract and repel—
never welcome the divine, and so,
nowhere more than out-there,

did the god twins feel more tossed aside
like the limbs
of a dismembered poet.

None of those celestial inexactitudes
traveled to was a place congenial—
there was no *there* to belong to,

nor existed a whenever when *when's*
inferred enough
they had a sense of whence—

or a longing to feel their own god-parts
with a sense of shame or abandonment—
and so, the god twins, reeling—feeling

turbulent and foul, need now the return
of some realm they must call home.

And since no common physic exists
to thin the urges gods have to require
their constant hysterias be spread
(like wild wisteria pinking the bones
of Phillips' folly)—
both twins entangle as one synchronous holy

noise—and it is by coin flip a choice is made,

choosing north is down and soon a re-ascendance
is anticipated—

then that slight anxiety felt about
which parishioners, if any, will have them
in lieu of their parochial god, Conneely,
about to go pale.

        And thusly, there is a row
to Pleasure Bay in the small armada of a dory.

        And in all their adjectival glory, be-decked
in lush rowdy regalia, each flashing a satin
-white burl of quartz set in pinky ring—

and imbedded with—as if in amber,
some soul-killing thing given by a god
of kills who was their neighbor
in the nethers;

they arrive at Nula's stoop and are as gods—
and are a plague of them.

        And while once Nula's foster of the archangel
in lieu of some bungle of a dreaming boy
had her imagine he was hers—

a redhead he's seen on Gold Street
has him dreamily imagining   the precious girl

        walking down the voluptuous street

Death Is Uniform in Its Sound

Whispers Conneely.

Nula feeds him with a spoon.

He's been gifted a twin's pinky ring, anonymously,
and biodegrades, mortally.

He cups his hand to his ear and claims to hear
the sea coming to drown him.

It is the seep of the reservoir, she says.

She wipes his mouth.

She summons apostate Watch & Warders to watch
over, unaware the god twins do its opposite—

and when those Bleeder ones come, they bleed him
under his tongue when night comes. And he fails.

And were it not for Michael, aloft, tracking the girl,
no one would smell the blood dump

clotting the night airs.
And the house empties as he appears.

And Conneely, wrongly,
sees him as the Angel of Death—

the archangel is noisy,
clips a chair with his foot as

he arrives in time for the whisper
of Conneely's soul needlessly shifting

from one vernacular toward another.

A Proper Language for the Celestial Hierarchy

or *Rules to be observed by The Natives of Ireland*
for Attaining a Just Pronunciation of English

Comes without wings. (A mother would have told him this.)

Comes with Latin flattening at the poles—
a sphere leaking to a hedron—
or the snorts of a horse he may or
may not have groomed at the H Street barn.

Or it comes by happenchance and its implied fuzzy
mathematicals with a life of their own—or it stunts
at the mouth unsaid, becomes that which

he could not find the words for.

And we excuse him for it.

And is that because the strong and weak forces
are neither at apogee or perigee—and thus
he's not inclined toward, nor does he lean to,
but is repelled by

those (   ) he is meant to nurture—be closest to?

And it doesn't matter that he's keenly intelligent,
or that he's once a boy observant and mentally alert.
Or that he wrongly imagines he is handy.

What matters is he's slow to show expressions of endearment—
a trait fossilized epochs ago. Ancient organic platelets turning

to stone

cause him to shift with that cosmos which

is his steel-toed father, his grandfather, et cetera,

        to this geology which is his,
ours.

The Precious Girl Walks Down the Voluptuous Street

Mother, what news it is
when you see him at his clumsy hover.

You, born the month they milk cattle thrice a day.

Father, born the month they turn children away—

or is it when the wagon horses are turned out to feed
in the meadow abounding the reservoir?

And are you mytho-logical?

Or is it as we see it plain—an ordinary husband and wife
and each of you (to the other) grown accustomed to,

and we safe as children—

the equation not losing its equilibrium,
our faces not painted toward ruin—

your simple language a mirror.

Couplets

He makes with her the shape of a heart—or wheel.
Not a memory wheel—but wagon wheels, four, on steel

staves—and bowed wooden boys—lagging, drawn by
a team of bays masked in feeder bags—the rag

-man yelling . . . *rags! Anyone got rags . . .*
and the coal man passing by without a pause

knowing any boys on this block kick their
coal from the tops of trains—

unless this is a false memory
washed in with a detritus

tide the day the butcher's helper died
out of the faint memory of his sons.

* * *

Meanwhile, Mikey has his hustles
and nocturnes—his brain box electric,

its foxy synapses behaving like stents in the narrows,
and widening Fort Point Channel enough that a few

eleventh century
ghosts—a sour-breathed ancient sept of his, slip

into Southie, past the sugar refinery, into
the Lower End at about the time the god twins

conduct their Irish Wake for Conneely—
out of respect for the newly dead king,

undead though he is, and that unbeknownst

to any but the archangel he mistook for Death,

and who, in that guise, takes Conneely's
breath for safe keep—or for keeps,

for all the sense there is to that theft since—
        god knows—he'll never grace the realm again.

Not Employed by God to Communicate His Will Toward Man

Nor are you the Angel of the Bottomless
Bottle
—or of Death. Bless-ed whisper, faint sound, dull
roar of wordless-ness who makes no sign.
—Oh, savior of breath; veiled

voice. Mis-speak. Say a few words
resounding. In dead Gaelic, if need be
—before we are deaf with incuriosity.

And when those wings, in wilt, appear
—wings in shape and form, poor foils
—not the special attributes

of a divine messenger. Why
do we expect so much of you
who are born of us

and mortal—and with your wounds
profound?

Father forgive a poor listener
attending to his own business

as you get on with your own.

Close by Blood and Neighborhood

To be good at fatherhood
is not a thing we knew from you.

And your father,
of the scornful look, the steel-toed shoe,

did not have the gift—

went mad with the lack of it—
not knowing what to do with sons.

What is it we got from you
endears us to—

has you more than blood and neighborhood—

the lowest orders of us flying,

not close, yet nearly so—
as a swirling murmuration

of starlings is intimate
so are we with you

in cold propinquity.

What Do Gods Teach

Archangel, why others
not us?

What do gods Teach
who leave us to ourselves?

What is god's Speech to us—
our familial god gone cold,

his wings thinned
to finger bones

reaching to others—not us

who want his wings
for swathe?

* * *

Why do our words fail—
our heart's voice quieter

than it ought be?

And what *hearts-ease*
there is

is discomforting.   This the threnody

the sixes and sevens sing to the body
impure

at St. Margaret's Parochial School.

This is the row they make
Grades 1 through 8—

an eight–oared boat rowing toward

what finish a finish makes.

Notes

I'LL GET TO THE CREATION STORY. . . : Includes excerpts from *The Random House Dictionary of the English Language,* Second Edition—used disagreeably.

OTHERS, AS THEY APPEAR: ". . . I can call spirits from the vastie deepe," is from Shakespeare's *Henry IV*, Part 1. The Irish king snake (see *Urban Dictionary*), a slang term for the large cock of a man of Irish descent—and which is said to be one of the nine powerful snakes from history and mythology.

HIERARCHICALS: ". . . the seal-boy—the aquanaut, Conneely," references West of Ireland lore which has it that the Conneely sept is descended from seals. See "Others, as They Appear" and "Feck, a God."

(SIX PLAIN COLOURLESS FACES): Adamantine is defined both as an adjective, meaning unbreakable, or a crystalline alicylic hydrocarbon . . . atoms arranged in three six-sided. . . . It is not a gemstone.

BAD LATIN: ". . .when midwives hibernate Souls for later," references the Southie fabrication that has Irish midwitches (midwives) emigrating to America, and who have the power to retrieve a Soul at a death, and place a Soul with a newborn. Apocryphal. Spurious. See irrational fears.

AETHER: On December 30, 1917, a convent asylum fire in Halifax, Nova Scotia, killed forty-five "insane" girls and one nun who tried to rescue them.

. . . WE WANT THEM TO SAY: St. Margaret's School was a Catholic parish elementary school in Dorchester, Massachusetts, attended by the author (see Sisters of Charity of Halifax in "Aether").

MUDDLE: Drill sergeants (some) are not as mean as they pretend to be.

LITTLE BANG CHAOS: "Eat of this!" A reference to Matthew 26:26, *King James Bible*, Oxford Edition, 1792, ". . . And as they were eating, Jesus took bread and bleſſed *it* and brake *it* and gave *it* to the diſciples, and ſaid, Take, eat; this is my body."

THE ENORMOUS: "God loves a cheerful giver. It says so in the book . . ." is part of a colloquy with a homeless man. Throughout the poem are references taken from the *Scientific American* article "Researchers Race to Rescue the Enormous Theorem before Its Giant Proof Disappears," July 1, 2015.

PROVOCATIVE MANIA: The L Street bathhouse is part of a Depression-era public beach complex on Dorchester Bay. Famed for its polar bear club, the "L Street Brownies," known, since 1902, for their New Year's Day swims.

THE HILL: The New England Watch and Ward Society was a later corruption of the New England Society for the Suppression of Vice founded in Boston in 1878.

SEND GOD: (see also "Row-a-Dory") Reference to the Phillips family of Ickford in the County of Bucks, is arbitrary, and has only to do with a Phillip's bookplate in the author's copy of *A Dictionary of the English Language,* Samuel Johnson, First Octavo Edition, 1756.

SCARY WALLPAPER DREAM: The italicized stanza "*If any of these marbles . . .*" is lifted from *The Office Professional's Guide,* Oxford University Press, 2003, p.124, and shows usage examples of indefinite pronouns.

OBLIVION: Definition from *Webster's Revised Unabridged Dictionary*, 1913. Cessation of remembrance; a kind of amnesty given the mind.

ANNATES: ". . . while Mikey first makes book . . ." He works for a bookie. The "T" is the Metropolitan Transit Authority (MTA) which is later absorbed by the Massachusetts Bay Transit Authority.

THE PRECIOUS GIRL WALKS DOWN THE VOLUPTUOUS STREET: The mother and father referenced in this poem are the author's. "You, born the month . . ." refers to the month of May. From the preface to *Bailey's Dictionarium Britannicum*, 1726, London. There is no reference to June as a month when they turn children away. They turned out cattle in June.

Dicko King was born at the old Carney Hospital in South Boston, and raised in St. Margaret's parish in Dorchester during the last of the grand and mythical eras presided over by tribes of feral children—when adventures could be had beyond the watchful eyes of a mother or father, and despite strictures and wounds inflicted by priest or nun. King's poems have appeared out of nowhere, some of them published in *Prime Number, Cactus Heart, Portland Review*, and *Straylight*. His first poetry book, *Doggerland: Ancestral Poems*, was a finalist for the Louise Bogan Award and won the Off the Grid Poetry Prize. His second book is *Bird Years* (Mayapple Press, 2017) and his novel, *The Book of Saves*, was longlisted for the YesYes Books 2023 Fiction Open.